Rookie
Read-About Science®

Animals under the Ground

By Allan Fowler

Consultants
Linda Cornwell, Learning Resource Consultant,
Indiana Department of Education

Fav Robinson, Child Development Specialist

4.95

Children's Press®
A Division of Grolier Publishing
New York   London   Hong Kong   Sydney
Danbury, Connecticut

Project Editor: Downing Publishing Services
Designer: Herman Adler Design Group
Photo Researcher: Caroline Anderson

Library of Congress Cataloging-in-Publication Data

Fowler, Allan.
    Animals under the ground / by Allan Fowler.
      p. cm. – (Rookie read-about science)
    Includes index.
    Summary: Briefly describes some of the animals that make their homes
under the ground, including moles, prairie dogs, and woodchucks.
    ISBN 0-516-20427-0 (lib.bdg.)   0-516-26254-8 (pbk.)
    1. Burrowing animals—Juvenile literature. 2. Soil animals—Juvenile
literature. [l. Burrowing animals. 2. Moles (Animals)] I. Title. II. Series
QL756.5.F68   1997   96-46946
591.757—dc21   CIP
                                                  AC

"You're making a mountain out of a molehill."

Did anyone ever say that to you? It means making a big fuss about something small or unimportant.

You know what a mountain is. But what's a molehill?

A mole is a mammal
that lives most of its life
underground. It is very
small — only about
6 inches long.

A mole has strong front
legs, with long claws.
It uses those claws to
dig tunnels.

One tunnel, about two feet underground, is the mole's home.

The mole lines this nest with leaves.

Shallower tunnels are for finding insects and worms to eat.

8

As the mole digs,
it piles up earth beside
the entrance to its tunnel.

And that pile of earth
is a molehill.

Moles can hardly see. Their
eyes are weak,
and are covered by fur.

But moles get along
very well in the dark.
They stay in their
tunnels, or burrows,
during the daytime.

If they come out at all,
it is usually at night.

12

Each day, a mole eats up to half its own weight in worms and insects.

Now *that's* hungry!

Can you imagine eating half *your* own weight every day?

Gophers also dig tunnels
and stay underground most
of the time. A gopher
might be a foot long,
larger than a mole.

Gophers and woodchucks are members of the rodent family, the same family of animals that includes mice and squirrels.

harvest mice

Woodchucks are sometimes called groundhogs.

During the winter months, when food is hard to find, they stay in their burrows.

They move around as little as they can, so they can live on just the food stored in their bodies.

This is called hibernating.

There's an old belief about February 2 — Groundhog Day.

If a woodchuck sees its shadow when it comes out of its burrow on that day, it will go right back inside — and winter will last another six weeks.

If the woodchuck doesn't see its shadow, then spring will come early. Of course, that's not true, but people like to pretend it is.

Woodchucks are about
two feet long.

Prairie dogs are a bit smaller. They bark like dogs, but are really a kind of squirrel.

Like moles, prairie dogs
leave mounds of earth
around the entrances
to the burrows they dig.

Unlike moles, prairie dogs
spend much time outdoors,
often sitting like this on
top of their mounds.

If one of them senses that a dangerous animal — or a human being — is near, it will whistle.

Then all the prairie dogs in the large colony will pop back into their holes, where most enemies can't follow them.

But animals called ferrets
sometimes do get into the
prairie dogs' tunnels —
and hunt the prairie dogs
for food.

Prairie dogs often live close together, in large groups. Their burrows might then seem like the "streets"of an underground "city."

Badgers belong to the same family of mammals as weasels. They dig burrows that may reach as deep as thirty feet under the earth.

Some rabbits live
underground.